This Spacious Place

Jan Cooper

O&U

Onwards & Upwards

Onwards and Upwards Publishers

3 Radfords Turf, Cranbrook, Exeter,
EX5 7DX, United Kingdom

www.onwardsandupwards.org

First edition, published in the United Kingdom by Onwards and Upwards Publishers Ltd. (2019).

ISBN:	978-1-78815-551-9
Typeface:	Sabon LT
Graphic design:	LM Graphic Design

Printed in the United Kingdom.

Endorsements

Like a butterfly emerging from a chrysalis, so has Jan's transformation taken her from a tightly bound, tormented soul to a woman totally set free to fly.

Her story is truly a message of hope and healing... Your spacious place is waiting!

Pastor Cathy Khan
Sonrise church, Hastings

Once when praying with Jan, the Holy Spirit gave a beautiful picture of the dawn with the rising sun. Jan's story is a testimony to the transforming love of Jesus and of the rays of His light bringing hope into dark places. Here is a reminder to us all of what the healing grace of God can do.

Revd Paul Deeming
Retired former missionary to Pakistan;
hospital chaplain, and a visiting chaplain at CCHC

About the Author

Jan Cooper is a qualified primary school teacher and has worked in both state and private schools during her teaching career, often working in learning support posts. She also gained an R.S.A. Diploma to teach pupils with specific learning difficulties, such as dyslexia. Although now retired, Jan still gives private tuition to a few pupils. Married to her husband Geoff, they have two grown-up children and two twin grandchildren.

Jan is actively involved in a local church in Hastings and especially enjoys being part of the Children's Church team. She also has a keen interest in worship dance and loves singing.

For several years now, Jan has been a prayer minister at Crowhurst Christian Healing Centre. As part of the ministry team there, they seek to help people find an intimate relationship with God the Father, His Son Jesus and to be equipped by the indwelling of the Holy Spirit to advance the Kingdom of God. In writing this book, Jan seeks to help people on their journey to wholeness, especially those who suffer with depression, which was her own experience.

Dedication

I dedicate this book to my family; my husband Geoff, my beautiful daughter Melanie and my amazing son Fraser, all of whom had to watch me suffer and who suffered much themselves during those years of my illness.

In Ephesians 3:20 we read:

> *Now to Him who is able to do immeasurably more than all we ask or imagine ... to Him be the glory.*

Our Heavenly Father can take all the broken pieces of our lives and, in His unending love and care, start to heal all those areas that are wounded or in deep pain. He gently puts us back together again and makes something truly beautiful.

Not only has the Lord performed such an amazing transformation in my life but also in the lives of Mel, Fraser and Geoff. I thought I had so damaged my family – but when the Lord restores, He restores thoroughly!

> *You will be a crown of splendour in the LORD's hand, a royal diadem in the hand of your God. No longer will they call you deserted or name your land desolate, but you will be called Hephzibah and your land Beulah; for the LORD will take delight in you...*
>
> *Isaiah 62:3-4*

This Spacious Place

Contents

This Spacious Place

Preface

Dear Friend,

As you read through my story you will become aware that at various times in my life I suffered severe depression and mental ill-health.

The main reason for writing this book is to give you hope if you too are suffering depression, mental ill-health or emotional difficulties. I want to share God's healing love and grace with you particularly.

In John 10:10 we read:

> *The thief comes only to steal and kill and destroy, I [Jesus] have come that they may have life and have it to the full.*

My prayer is that as you read my book you will come to know how much you are loved by God – how precious, how special, how unique you are. I pray that your life, like mine, will be utterly transformed to become the beautiful person that our loving Heavenly Father designed you to be, and that you will stand tall and confident knowing who you are 'in Christ'.

To Him be the glory!

> *The King is enthralled by your beauty, honour Him for He is your Lord.*
>
> *Psalm 45:11*

May you marvel when you realise that the Lord of all creation loves you and is longing to enjoy an intimate relationship with you!

The Priestly Blessing

The LORD bless you and keep you;
The LORD make his face shine upon you
And be gracious to you;
The LORD turn his face towards you
And give you peace.

Numbers 6:24-26

God bless you!

Jan

CHAPTER ONE

Early Childhood Memories

I WAS BORN ON 20TH SEPTEMBER, 1948, IN NEWBURY, Royal Berkshire. My parents were Edith Annie and Maurice Hugh Townsend, and I have an elder sister, Pam, who still lives in Newbury. My parents were Christians and I remember my childhood to be very happy.

When I was four years old, my parents bought a small-holding of three-and-a-half acres and we lived in a bungalow in Cromwell Road, Shaw, Newbury. My father was a pork butcher and whilst he was at work, my mother looked after the orchard and the animals as well as looking after my sister, me and Grandad Smith, who lived with us.

I absolutely adored my father and spent much time with him on the small-holding. We had three sows, hundreds of chickens (free range), some turkeys, a cockerel, some rabbits, and sometimes we let people graze their horses in our orchard of apple and pear trees – and even a friend's donkey, Bella. We also had a beautiful golden retriever dog called Webster.

Whenever our sows were giving birth, I helped my dad. One sow, Sarah, used to become very distressed. We had to board up her sty, pad it with lots of straw and literally try to catch the little piglets as Sarah birthed them. Then we had to keep them from her until she had finished giving birth, to protect them until she had calmed down. Another sow, Sue, always bore too many piglets and we tried to rear them in our kitchen, with varying success.

Our kitchen had a tiled floor, a Rayburn cooker and a 'copper' in the corner. Wash day, Monday, was always particularly busy. I remember my mother having to work very hard and I know she was often in pain because she had an extreme curvature of the spine.

We were brought up to go to church, Newbury Baptist. I sang my first solo in church when I was just four years old. We went to Sunday School every Sunday afternoon and my mum played the piano. The Sunday School was large, and we studied for scripture exams there. I also played in a recorder group, and went to Girls Brigade where, again, my mum played the piano for our worship times and our country dancing.

At one time my dad bought an old van, even though he couldn't drive (a friend, Robin, used to drive). Every Saturday we cleaned out the van, put some seats in and then on Sunday we drove some of our neighbours' children to Sunday School with us.

We used to have a Sunday School outing every year to Hayling Island. We loved going on a coach for a day at the seaside. One year, when I was perhaps eight or nine years old, I was staying with my nan and grandad Townsend, who were going to take me on the coach. But on the morning of the trip, I fell down the last three stairs coming down to breakfast. I really hurt my shoulder but told Nan I was fine because I didn't want to miss a day at the seaside. When it came to putting on my swimming costume at the beach, though, I couldn't raise my shoulder and it was so painful I started to cry. My nan then realised I had really injured myself when I fell down the stairs. The next day, Mum and Dad took me to the hospital, where the diagnosis was a 'green-stick' fracture of my shoulder – and my arm ended up in a sling for six weeks.

I attended Speenhamland Primary School. My headmaster was Mr Watts and one of the members of our church, Miss Fisher, was my reception class teacher. It was a good school. My father used to walk with me to school, a journey of two-and-a-half miles. He would wheel his bicycle along, then leave me in the school playground and cycle off to work.

My sister, being six years older than me, went to Newbury County Girls' Grammar School whilst I was at primary. One Monday she had a holiday and I didn't. I went very reluctantly to school with my dad that morning! Once there, we had to take our dinner money tin, put it on our desk and then go out to play. Having done this, I felt a great injustice that I should have to be at school whilst my sister was at home! So when no-one was looking, I sneaked out of the playground and started my long walk back! About three-quarters of the way home, I saw my neighbour, Mrs Fiddler, coming out of a local shop. She asked what I was doing, to which I replied, 'I'm not very well and they've sent me home from school'! I quite expected my mum to be pleased to see me. How wrong could I be! Mum was busy doing the washing in the old 'copper' when I entered the kitchen. Of course, she was really cross, turned off the 'copper', put her coat on and took me straight back to school. I was crying and protesting most of the way but there was worse to come... My class teacher had found my dinner money tin on my desk but then had not been able to find me! The headmaster had telephoned my father at work and he had said he'd left me in the playground. Horrors! Where was I? Mr Watts picked me up, stood me on the teacher's table and told the whole class what a very naughty girl I had been. They had all been so worried about me... I was only six years old at the time.

On a happier note, I also remember sports days at Speenhamland Primary School. I was good at sport and won lots of prizes and certificates. I was a tall girl and was very good at the high jump as well as a very fast runner. I was also very successful at the 'slow-bicycle' race but hated the sack race!

My primary school years were very happy, and I passed my 11+ exam, which enabled me to attend Newbury County Girls' Grammar School in 1960.

Chapter Two

My Senior School Years

WHEN I WAS ELEVEN YEARS OLD, MY PARENTS SOLD the small-holding for building land and we moved into a lovely bungalow overlooking Victoria Park in Newbury, a very pleasant position. Our bungalow was called Home Close. We had a huge garden and my father continued to grow many vegetables and flowers.

My mother enjoyed two years of a less hectic lifestyle, until my father, who was quite an entrepreneur, decided he wanted to buy a friend's business, the Rainbow Café in Bartholomew Street, Newbury! So we rented out our bungalow and moved into a flat over the café. On moving day, my father had fallen ill with the flu and was in bed with a very high temperature. The removal men packed up everything around him, while he was left in bed until the very last minute, then was put to bed in the flat as soon as possible. The lion's share of the hard work then fell on my mother's shoulders and she had to begin running the café without my father's help for the first few weeks. When my father finally recovered, my mother collapsed with nervous exhaustion and was in bed for about three weeks. She was very poorly, and my sister and I had to help my father until she recovered.

The café was extremely busy and although my parents employed staff, it was very hard work. I spent part of my summer holidays washing up in the kitchen; we didn't have a dishwasher in the 1960s! Some summer days were really hot and the temperature in the kitchen soared to an unbearable heat. Often I felt very faint and had to go upstairs to rest for a while before returning back to work.

We all began to miss being able to sit and relax in a garden and I know my mother wished she were back in the bungalow at Victoria Park. It was a very difficult time, and after three years my parents decided to sell the café and we moved back to Home Close, where life became less stressful again.

By this time my sister had started her nursing training at Hammersmith Hospital in London, while I continued to work hard at my grammar school. I was quite artistic but because the school were hoping that I would go to university, I had to give up Art and take up Latin! I tried for two years to enjoy Latin, but I didn't succeed and eventually gave it up. By this time, however, it was too late to take Art O level.

I studied hard for my O level exams but found it stressful and lost about half a stone in weight. At first 'sitting' I gained seven O levels and then took another 4 exams which gave me eleven in total.

I was then accepted for my teacher training at Eastbourne College of Education without any A levels but had studied one year of the English Literature A level syllabus.

Summing up my teenage years, I didn't enjoy my grammar school. Some of the teachers were quite harsh and I was a rather sensitive person who had to work very hard to achieve academic success. I enjoyed playing tennis and lacrosse but wasn't so keen on cricket – my position in fielding was either 'silly mid-on' or 'silly mid-off'' – well-named because it could be quite dangerous.

On my eighteenth birthday, I began my teacher training course at Eastbourne. I arrived with my family to find that my room in Queenswood would be home for four of us – Josie, Karen, Barbara and me – with other girls in rooms further along the corridor. I put my birthday cards up on my dressing table and then had to say goodbye to my family. Fortunately, Josie immediately became like a mother figure to me, although she was only a year older than me. She looked after me and we became really good friends, and although we don't see one another very often anymore, we still remain close.

I had been baptised when I was sixteen years old at Newbury Baptist Church and used to enjoy helping with the children's holiday clubs we used to organise. I also became a Sunday School teacher. Here I wanted to go to church too, and my cousin Michael, who had become a Baptist minister, recommended I try Victoria Drive Baptist Church. So one evening I went with a friend from college to a service and afterwards I found myself coming down the steps of the church wondering if we should go to the young people's after-church get-together.

Then it happened!... At the top of the steps I noticed a very handsome young man coming out of church – and he smiled at me!

That decided it. 'We are going to the after-church get-together,' I announced to my friend!

We were given a lift by the pastor's son to someone's home and for about an hour and a half I sat there 'spellbound', looking at and listening to this amazing person whose name was Geoff! I learned that he had just returned to Eastbourne that August after being in a professional band in Germany for a year as a drummer and was now living with his parents for a while. I now knew it was possible to fall in love at first sight!

I went back to my college room that night on 'cloud nine'. Geoff had given my friend and me a lift home and I couldn't stop talking about this fantastic guy I'd just met!

Geoff and I kept seeing one another. All my friends were jealous as I was the first one to fall in love and I hadn't even had to go to a college dance to find my man… One evening they were going to the cinema to see *The Sound of Music,* starring Julie Andrews, and I asked if Geoff would like to come. That evening, all my friends were looking to see if we were holding hands!

When the film ended, Geoff asked if I'd like to go to his home to meet his parents and I said yes. He had an old black Ford 8 car, and as we started to drive off, Geoff realised we had run out of petrol, so we had to walk to a garage, fill a petrol can up, put it in the car and then make our way to his home. Geoff's parents welcomed me and wanted to give me some supper; I asked them for toast and dripping! They were Christians and were members of Victoria Drive Baptist Church. They were lovely and made me so welcome. Geoff's father was completely deaf but could lip-read and we got on very well.

Geoff and I both believed God had brought our lives together. We were so in love, and by Easter 1967 we had become engaged! Geoff travelled home to Newbury with me to ask my father if he could marry me. My dear father said, 'Yes, Geoff, I give you my blessing to marry Jan, but she must finish her college course and her probationary teaching year first.' So we knew our engagement would be a long one. Very excitedly we made a trip to Oxford Street in London where I chose my beautiful engagement ring in Ratners. It is a solitaire diamond with a lover's knot; we were told it was unique and I have never seen an identical one. In 1967 it cost £25!

CHAPTER THREE

My College Years

I WAS TRAINING TO BE A PRIMARY SCHOOL TEACHer. My main subject was Theology and my second subject, Movement and Dance Drama. I'm not sure whether my Theology tutors were Christians; my main tutor certainly made us think and question everything. I was a young Christian and didn't know how to respond to questions like, 'If God is a God of love, why does He require a blood sacrifice before He will forgive sins?' I know that my cousin Michael was praying for me that I wouldn't lose my faith, but I did start to question everything. That isn't a bad thing in itself, but my faith did start to 'wobble' after a while. Nonetheless, I went to the Christian Union meetings and actually became the prayer secretary.

My first teaching practice was at an infants' school in Rye. The practice was for four weeks and I was in a reception class. I began to realise that I had led quite a sheltered life and didn't expect five-year-olds could be so challenging! I didn't find my class teacher or headmistress to be helpful at all, either. There were thirty-two children in the class, I believe, and I didn't cope at all well. I found it very difficult to keep discipline and sometimes found myself going into the 'loo' and crying. I hated it! My friend Margo, whose father was a headmaster, was doing so well in her practice, while I felt a complete failure! Geoff drove over to the 'digs' Margo and I were sharing with a teacher in Winchelsea, to see me and encourage me.

At the end of the practice I went to the college principal, Miss Hitchens, and asked to leave. However, she wouldn't give her permission and said they thought I would make a good teacher one day. They did place me in a better school for my second teaching practice at Crowborough, but I still thought I'd probably made a wrong career choice, and just wanted to give it all up and marry Geoff.

In those days we had to be in college by 10.30pm. We were allowed some late passes to be in by 11.15pm and a couple of late, late passes each term to be in by midnight. One day Geoff and I were just talking in his car outside Queenswood, when I suddenly realised it was gone midnight and I hadn't asked for a late pass! Geoff threw some stones up at the window of my room, where my friends were all wondering where I was. They tried to creep down to open the front door for me, only to meet Miss Hitchens in the hallway. Oh no! I was reprimanded – but I was in love, didn't she realise?

My third teaching practice was at Goudhurst. I actually gained a 'merit' there, but still didn't really enjoy being a class teacher.

I very much enjoyed my second subject, Movement and Dance Drama. I'd never been taken to dancing lessons as a child but found 'moving' very liberating. My tutor, Miss Platt, was very encouraging and clearly saw potential in me. Once I went to a Dance/Drama weekend at Crystal Palace and loved it. Miss

Platt wanted me to apply to gain a place at the Laban School of Movement and Dance/Drama, but that would have meant another year to wait before Geoff and I could marry so I declined. I have, however, always maintained my interest in, and love of, dance and drama, and at various times in my Christian life have been involved in worship dance.

———————

During my first and third year at college, I was in 'halls' at Queenswood. In our second year some friends and I were in 'digs' in a guesthouse near Eastbourne pier. My friend Joy and I shared a room which overlooked the sea! It was, however, a long journey to college each morning. At the time, Geoff had a driving job with Louis G. Ford in Eastbourne. Some mornings, as my friends and I were making our way to college, we would see Geoff's work van approaching. Then he would stop and give me a lift to college. Prior to this, Geoff had been working as a deckchair attendant on Eastbourne seafront in the summer months, and in the winter repairing the deckchairs.

———————

At this point, a bit of Geoff's story will help to paint a wider picture. On leaving Eastbourne Grammar School at age sixteen, he had gone into the Westminster bank and had shown some early promise having come top of his class at the bank's college in Oxford. However, playing the drums was becoming a big part of his life; the band he played in won a national competition so they decided to turn professional and do it full time. This meant leaving the bank, and the band moved to London. They played all over the country, alongside many top groups of that era as well as spending a good while playing in clubs all over Germany.

The band, called Shelley, made four or five records, one of which made it to No. 49 in the English pop charts. The band appeared on several TV programmes, including Juke Box Jury, and radio programmes such as Saturday Club.

However, whilst in Hamburg playing in the Star-Club where the Beatles had performed, Geoff experienced God speaking to him in a very clear and powerful way. God told Geoff that He wanted him back in England because He had new plans for him, although those new plans didn't become clear to him for some while.

So Geoff left the band and came back to England. He was replaced by another drummer and Shelley went on to have a No. 1 hit in Denmark. However, the band eventually folded and individual members went their separate ways. Incidentally, Geoff has carried on drumming most of his life but in the different environment of worship bands in church settings.

Back in England whilst waiting for God's plans to unfold, Geoff had been doing the driving job and working as a deckchair attendant. Then, after about two years, he felt called to go into the YMCA and following a six-month placement at Ipswich YMCA, he went to the YMCA National College in Walthamstow as a full-time mature student, to train as a Youth and Community Worker.

Before Geoff went off to Ipswich we bought an amazing red MG TC sports car from a friend of mine in Newbury. Then my college friends were *really* envious of me being met by my handsome fiancé in his MG TC. No – actually, they were very happy for me. But after about a year, the petrol tank at the back developed a leak (amongst other things) and we didn't have the money to have it repaired so we sadly had to sell the car. We were very disappointed.

In 1969, I left college and went back home to live with my parents in Newbury in order to begin my probationary year teaching at Francis Bailey Primary School in Thatcham, just three miles from Newbury. My father bought me a little Mini after I had passed my driving test when I was seventeen years old. I was to teach a reception class of thirty children.

I found my first term very difficult, particularly as some of the children had significant special educational needs, and I felt very stressed. By the Christmas holidays I was in a state of breakdown. Geoff, at this point, was still training at Walthamstow. He used to write at least two letters a week, trying to encourage me. My parents, also, were very supportive but I really didn't feel at all confident and wanted to give up teaching. My mum took me to our family GP, who prescribed one week's tranquillisers in order to help me relax and get some sleep, telling me I would be fine!

The New Year came, 1970. Geoff and I were to be married in August. I didn't know how I was going to manage another two terms of teaching in order to get my qualification. I think the only thing that kept me going was preparing for our wedding.

My mum and I went up to London in the Easter holidays and bought the material for my wedding dress and my sister's bridesmaid dress, and I chose my beautiful veil. Then each week I worked on my dress. My mum had always been good at needlework and had taught me, and I enjoyed making our dresses and sending out invitations for our wedding on August 8th.

I had actually decided that after Geoff and I were married, I would not teach anymore but think of a different career path. So I was very surprised to hear that I had passed my probationary year teaching and was an accredited primary school teacher.

CHAPTER FOUR

Wedding and Early Married Life

Family at the wedding

AUGUST 8TH FINALLY CAME – A GLORIOUS, SUNNY day. Geoff and I were married at Newbury Baptist Church at 1.30pm. We then had a wonderful reception in the church hall for all our family and friends who had come from many places across the country. A hundred guests enjoyed a sit-down meal.

Jan and her father

My sister's father-in-law, who had worked as chief gardener for the Parker Bowles family, had worked very hard to make the church and church hall beautiful with amazing floral displays. He had been helped by Mrs Mitchell, our minister's wife. She had sprayed bicycle baskets gold and filled them with the most amazing flowers. It was such a beautiful day and I felt so happy as Geoff and I drove off in my little Mini which had been 'decorated' by my college friends and Geoff's brother Tezz whilst we were in the reception.

We made our way to Eastleigh airport to catch our flight to Jersey where we were to spend our honeymoon. Cars kept beeping their horns at us because we had 'Just Married' written all over our car – I loved it.

Geoff and Jan on their wedding day

We arrived at our hotel in St Brelade's Bay. I remember opening our case in our room, only to find that Josie had 'stuffed confetti' everywhere which, as I unpacked my clothes, went all over the carpet. Geoff immediately began to collect it all up. I didn't understand why he did that though, because I wanted everyone to know that we were just married! We enjoyed a lovely week in Jersey and hired a red MG sports car so we could see the whole island. The weather was mostly sunny and warm, and Geoff and I were together, married at last.

Just a few weeks after our honeymoon we moved to Ipswich, where Geoff began his career in the YMCA as a youth worker and I found a job at the Ipswich hospital as a nursing auxiliary. Our first home belonged to someone connected with Ipswich YMCA. It was a terraced house on the busy Norwich Road just a few doors down from the main YMCA building. We had been told it would be decorated before we moved in but that hadn't happened. Geoff and I went out and bought brightly coloured paints. Our hallway became yellow and orange with a purple front door and we chose lime-green and white to paint other doors!

The realities of life soon started to kick in. Geoff was working with very challenging young people, including some in the residential accommodation that had mental health issues, and I was finding my work as an auxiliary nurse very tough. As a newly married couple we soon found ourselves in the deep end, with very little support.

Fortunately, the YMCA Regional Secretary Ray Onions and his wife Alice invited us to lunch with them one Sunday.

Alice was the deputy head at Dale Hall primary school in Ipswich. When she learned that I was a qualified teacher but had lost my confidence, she asked if I would like to consider a full-time post at Dale Hall as a Learning Support teacher working with small groups throughout the day. I decided to take the opportunity and started working in the spring term of 1971. I had my own small room and my groups were not more than six children at any one time. I loved it. I had found my niche.

One afternoon Geoff met me from work and said, 'I hope you don't mind but Jimmy is coming to live with us.' Jimmy had been brought up in children's homes for most of his life. He had got into trouble and Geoff had gone to court with him. If Geoff hadn't offered for Jimmy to live with us, he may have been sent to a young offenders' institution. We had only been married for six months, but I really liked Jimmy so I didn't mind. Nonetheless, it did prove to be very challenging!

Eventually Jimmy found himself in serious trouble and was sent to a young offenders' institution. We had tried to help him and we visited Jimmy in borstal but there wasn't much else we could do. We were sure we had made a positive impact on his life, though, and hoped that the positive experiences we had given him would prove helpful later on.

About a year later, Geoff had another surprise for me. He met me from school and told me he had just bought a house for us. It had been a little 'two up and two down' property but the previous owners had built a large extension and it was decorated well throughout. It also had a large garden to the rear of the property. We were very excited and moved into the first home of our own – and lived there for just eight weeks...

Geoff had found his job increasingly demanding and was unhappy in his work so he applied for another post in Devon which was Torbay YMCA. It was a youth and community centre with great facilities and he was successful in his application. So in October 1972 we moved to Paignton and bought a little two-bedroom bungalow in Eden Grove. I started teaching at the nearby Foxhole Infant School as a part-time learning support teacher and Geoff managed the Clennon Valley YMCA centre. Amongst other things, Geoff built up a strong canoe club there, making their own fibreglass canoes. He taught many young people how to canoe and became a very experienced white-water canoeist himself.

––––––––––––

Geoff and I began to want to start a family. It wasn't happening for us, however, so we sought help and I was given some hormone treatment to help me conceive. In the summer of 1974, I became pregnant. At first, I was very excited but about four months into the pregnancy my feelings turned to fear – not of the physical birth but the whole weight of responsibility of becoming a mother; it just overwhelmed me. No-one could teach me how to become a good mother. I just didn't know what to do and I didn't feel able to talk to Geoff or anyone about my fears.

About this time, I had started to go to a Bible study with my neighbour Peggy at her Anglican church. Rev. Gel, who ran it, was an older, Spirit-filled minister. I loved listening to him explaining Bible passages. In fact, most of the people were much older than me (I was only twenty-five) but I loved hearing them pray and they made me feel very loved and accepted.

One evening most people had gone home and I overheard Rev. Gel say to a small group of ladies, 'Someone here is very afraid.'

I just burst into tears and said, 'It's me!'

Rev. Gel asked if I would like them to pray with me and I replied, 'Yes, please!'

So the ladies made a circle around me, and Rev. Gel placed his hands on my head and told me they were going to ask the Holy Spirit to fill me. One lady was given a prophecy for me which was, 'My peace I give unto you. My grace I give unto you. I will protect you from all harm and danger. Trust me, My child.'

Although I had been brought up in church for most of my life, I hadn't really understood that I was God's child. That night I walked home with Peggy on 'cloud nine'. The fear had gone, and I knew something beautiful had happened to me! God had filled me with His Spirit.

Rev. Gel came to visit me a couple of days later and had some verses for me (Hebrews 13:20-21): '...may the God of peace, who through the blood of the eternal covenant brought back from the dead our Lord Jesus, that great Shepherd of the sheep, equip you with everything good for doing his will and may he work in us what is pleasing to him, through Jesus Christ, to whom be glory for ever and ever. Amen.'

For the rest of my pregnancy I felt very close to God. Then on April 5th, 1975, I started in labour. As I was considered 'older' for a first pregnancy (aged twenty-six years), I was booked into Torbay Hospital for the birth. At 10.30pm my waters broke so Geoff telephoned the hospital and they said to come in. It was just a short journey from our home in Paignton and we arrived at midnight. I was examined, and the sister said our baby probably wouldn't be born until the morning, so Geoff left me at 2am and went home for some sleep. I was given a sleeping tablet and fell fast asleep until about 4am, when I woke to realise the rest of my waters had broken. I called the sister and she examined me and said, 'Your baby is going to be born very soon!'

I wanted Geoff to be with me for the birth, so they telephoned him but couldn't wake him at first. I said, 'Keep on ringing!' Finally, he was woken, and he arrived at the hospital just after 4.30am. Melanie Ruth, our beautiful daughter, was born ten minutes later! It had been an almost pain-free birth and I felt so happy and grateful to God.

I was transferred the next day to the little cottage hospital in Paignton, which was lovely. I was in a little two-bed ward. The babies there were looked after at night in the nursery and the nurses had plenty of time to help us with our babies and breast-feeding and showed us how to bath our babies. I was able to have a week in hospital and I felt so close to God. It was a special time for me. I believed that God had kept His beautiful promise of protection given me in the prophecy when I was four months pregnant. I didn't feel at all tired and I was communing with my Heavenly Father without words. Then, when I looked in the mirror, I saw that my face was shining with the glory of the Lord. When I looked out of the window, the light looked much brighter than usual. It was a very heightened spiritual experience, almost like being in Heaven.

After seven days I was allowed to go home and although it was April, it had been snowing during the week. So we made our little bungalow cosy and warm and started life as a family.

Up to this point, I hadn't received much teaching on the work of the Holy Spirit. Geoff and I were worshiping at a local Baptist church, so we weren't part of Rev. Gel's congregation. When the special spiritual experience started to fade, I thought quite wrongly that God had left me and that now I was on my own.

———————

At first, I thought I was doing quite well as a mum but as time went on, I found that I was missing my teaching. Geoff was working long hours at the YMCA and because I didn't have any relatives living near, I began to feel lonely and isolated and started to slip into depression. I hadn't been told that some women suffer quite severe postnatal depression. Melanie was a beautiful baby and I loved her very much, so I kept thinking that soon I would feel a lot better. I kept looking after Melanie but wasn't looking after myself very well, and by not eating much, I started losing weight. Sometimes I would make an appointment to see my GP but then would cancel it.

Melanie was around eighteen months old, I believe, when my sister came to stay for a little holiday with us. My sister quickly realised that I was very unwell and told Geoff he must take me to see our doctor. At first, I was prescribed anti-depressant tablets, but then it was suggested that I attend a clinic in Torquay as a day patient for three weeks. Geoff's parents came to stay, to look after Melanie whilst I was at the clinic. Geoff used to drive me to Torquay, leave me there and then pick me up at about 4pm.

I found the whole experience very frightening! I think I was the only mum suffering from postnatal depression. Other patients were experiencing all kinds of mental health difficulties and some were very ill indeed. I hated it.

I had to attend group therapy sessions. One day, one of the nurses said to me, 'You keep smiling but are you really happy?'

I just broke down in tears and said, '*No,* I'm really *un-*happy.'

By this time, I was very thin. I then had to see the psychiatrist because of my response to the nurse, and Geoff was called in. I couldn't wait for the three weeks to end.

After that, I tried hard to feel better as I never wanted to go to that clinic again. This period of struggling with depression lasted several years and although Geoff and I still went to church, I wasn't able to draw any strength or help from my faith and again didn't know how to receive God's love.

My parents obviously felt very concerned, as did Geoff's parents, but it was difficult for them to help as we lived in Paignton and they lived in Newbury and Eastbourne, respectively. I did, however, from time to time go to stay for a while with them.

CHAPTER FIVE

Moving On – 1980

MELANIE STARTED SCHOOL AND I THOUGHT PER-
haps I should find a teaching post. I was too afraid to consider
having another baby due to my previous postnatal depression,
but again I had lost confidence concerning teaching.

We then started going to a different church with some
friends, Hele Road Baptist Church in Torquay. Our pastors
John and Jackie were lovely, and I began to feel more settled.
With time I even began to think that perhaps I would like to
have another baby. I really did want Melanie to have a brother
or sister. Geoff and I decided that I wouldn't have any more
hormone treatment to help me conceive but we would just see
what happened naturally...

I became pregnant again in April 1982. Geoff was beginning
to feel he needed a new challenge as we had been at Torbay
YMCA for almost eleven years. That summer Geoff went for
interviews at Portsmouth YMCA and then Hastings and was
offered the post of General Secretary at Hastings YMCA.

In early October we moved to Sussex when I was about
seven-and-a-half months pregnant. We had sold our home in
Paignton but as we hadn't had time to find a home in Hastings,
we were given temporary accommodation in a council 'key
worker' house for six months. I thought I would have six weeks

to prepare for the birth of our second child but actually went into labour three weeks after we arrived.

Fraser Hugh was born on December 6th, 1982. Melanie was seven years old and now had a brother.

Fraser's birth was not an easy one, but he was beautiful and this time I suffered no depression, even though we were living in temporary accommodation in a different town where we didn't know anyone apart from one or two people connected with the YMCA. Melanie loved her baby brother and soon settled into the junior department of her new school, Blacklands. We were, however, also now near Geoff's parents in Eastbourne and we enjoyed spending time with them quite regularly.

Within six months we had moved into our own home at Holly Bank Gardens. We started attending the Elim church in Hastings and became friends with our pastor Ivan Potts and his wife Margaret. Their ministry helped Geoff and me understand God's grace in a deeper way. I became a Sunday School teacher and later took on the responsibility of leading the children's work. I also began to write Bible stories for children which were recorded professionally in a studio, and I think we sold about two hundred story tapes, the money raised going to the Elim church in Hastings. Geoff began drumming in the worship group and it became a happy time for us as a family. Melanie was baptised, and I started a ladies' keep fit class on Monday evenings at the church; Melanie and Fraser used to enjoy coming with me and taking part. I also helped with the church playgroup three mornings a week, which Fraser enjoyed.

Life seemed to be going well but then Geoff started to feel extremely tired. He always worked long hours at the YMCA and at first thought that was the reason for his tiredness. However, when the tiredness began to be complete exhaustion, we sought help from our GP. At first, Geoff was not understood, but then a new GP came to our practice. He was kind and sympathetic toward him and decided to run blood tests to see if he had Chronic Fatigue Syndrome. The tests showed that Geoff had a virus which he may have contracted when he was a keen canoeist in Devon and the virus had remained in Geoff's body causing chronic fatigue. There was no medication the GP could give him but the fact that Geoff had been listened to and given a diagnosis of M.E. actually helped him significantly.

Geoff was able to take three months off work but then had to return and take up his duties again. It was a very difficult time, as he had to manage the YMCA and the long hours of work that entailed. I would often get a phone call from him saying, 'I've hit the wall.' So I would encourage him to come home for a rest, where he would sit in a chair and immediately fall asleep. Later, I would wake him for his meal and then, after about an hour, he would often have to return to the YMCA for the evening sessions, not arriving home until about 11pm.

Geoff's sleep pattern was interrupted, he experienced severe muscle cramps, concentration became difficult and he experienced other distressing symptoms associated with M.E. The extreme exhaustion was very difficult to deal with. We believe he had M.E. for about twelve years.

———————

In August 1990, Geoff and I and Melanie and Fraser were on holiday in Cornwall when we received a phone call from my sister to say Mum was in hospital in Reading following a heart attack. Mum had said she didn't want us to break our holiday but the next day we packed up and travelled to Newbury arriving at my sister's home late afternoon on a Monday. We wanted to go straight to the hospital to see my mother but my father and sister had been visiting her that afternoon and said that she seemed a lot better but would probably be too tired for any more visitors that day. Instead, then, we went to my parents' home and began to unpack.

At about 6.30pm we received a phone call from the hospital to say that Mum had suffered another heart attack and we ought to come. My father and I travelled in my sister's car to Reading, which was seventeen miles from Newbury, while Geoff stayed at home to look after Mel and Fraser. As I sat in the back of the car, I looked up at the skies and prayed. I felt the Lord gently say to me, 'Your mother is with me.'

When we arrived at the hospital, the doctor took us aside and told us that Mum had just died even though they had tried everything they could. I had never seen a dead person before and now I had to go and see my mother. As we went into the room, my father knelt at my mother's bedside crying. My sister was also crying, but I felt as if I were in a bubble or cocoon of God's love. The Lord was surrounding me with His loving presence and I knew my mother was in Heaven; her body was an empty shell now and I was happy she was out of all her pain.

I found a strength and comfort in those days after my mother's death and I knew it was the Lord. I found that I was able to comfort my father. I was almost forty-two years old at this point, while Melanie was fifteen and Fraser seven.

The funeral was arranged quickly, and we held a service at Newbury Baptist church to which many people came. My mother had been a very faithful wife and mother and had walked humbly with her Lord. She hadn't sought the limelight but had always been busy in the background.

My mother was then buried in Shaw cemetery.

I didn't doubt that she was now in Heaven and for the first few months after her death I was just so pleased she was there. She had not enjoyed good health throughout her lifetime, but she hadn't complained and instead just got on with life and worked very hard, touching the lives of many others.

I felt very close to God again.

One day I visited a friend of mine who had breast cancer. I had met Pat in the school playground because her youngest daughter was in the same class as Fraser and we had been taking her to Sunday School with us. Pat had had a mastectomy and wanted to show me. I felt the Lord's compassion flood through me and I asked her if I could pray for her. She was very happy for me to do so. I explained that I was going to pray 'in the name of Jesus'. Then I gently laid my hands on her shoulders and started to pray.

After a short while Pat said, 'Oh, don't stop praying, Jan. I can feel heat coming through your hands!'

I couldn't feel any heat but knew it was Jesus touching her, so I just explained that to her and kept praying.

Pat subsequently had to have her other breast removed and went through chemotherapy. Pat noticed that I was wearing a cross, which was actually my mother's cross that my father had given me after her death. She asked if she could borrow it to hold in the night when fears sometimes overwhelmed her. So I gave her the cross and I knew it gave her comfort during those dark days and nights.

After a few months my father came to stay with us for a holiday and as he walked through the door on his own, my grief suddenly hit and I started to cry. I wanted my father to just hold me and let me cry but he never liked to see us upset and said, 'Don't cry, Jan!'

That visit was difficult for me, as when I needed to cry, I would rush up to the bedroom or bathroom so that Dad didn't see me. Then after a while, I would splash my face with cold water and try to hide the fact. After my father went home, I found that I was crying a lot and probably should have sought some bereavement counselling but again thought the grief would just ease in time.

My father was living in his bungalow in Newbury. He was near his church and the town and enjoyed his beautiful garden. I thought he would be best to stay there and buy in any help he needed as money wasn't a problem. Geoff and I were very happy to have him come to stay with us for regular holidays and we would visit him some weekends at Newbury. My sister, however, wanted to move into his bungalow with her family in order to look after him. I wasn't at all sure this would be wise, and tensions began to appear whilst they were living together. After about a year my father decided to buy a flat in a block very near to the bungalow, which eased the tension in relationships. He seemed to settle quite happily and lived there in the flat for the rest of his life. He died three years after my mother's death, in August 1993. He had suffered his first heart attack when I was expecting Melanie and I wasn't sure then if he would live to see our first child, but he did. He subsequently had three more heart attacks during his lifetime but reached the age of 78 years. He wasn't able to survive his final heart attack but Geoff, my sister, my cousin Michael and I were at his bedside when he died. A few minutes before, he told us he was with Mum in a beautiful garden – reunited in Heaven.

My father's funeral took place at Newbury Baptist church, to which many people came, and then he was buried alongside my mother at Shaw Cemetery.

When I visit my parents' grave, I often remember how, when we owned the small-holding which bordered the cemetery, our pigs broke down the fence and decided to wander around! We had to quickly round them up and guide them safely back into the orchard. My father then had to make our fence more secure...

I was almost forty-five years old when my father died.

CHAPTER SIX

The Mid-Life Years and Beyond

MID-LIFE CRISIS? THE MENOPAUSE? OFTEN THESE are quite difficult years, as our parents become unwell and death becomes a reality at a time when perhaps we don't feel so well ourselves. I began the menopausal years at thirty-eight, which is quite young, and when hormones are not in balance they can affect us quite severely. Also, our children may be going through their teenage struggles and life can be quite challenging. It certainly was for us as a family.

In her late teens and early twenties Melanie got very 'lost'. As parents, Geoff and I became very concerned about her welfare but didn't really know how best to help. I began to think it was all my fault, that I hadn't been a good enough mother. I do believe that Melanie had not felt very secure in her very early years when I had suffered severe postnatal depression and I felt this to be one of many contributing factors as our relationship began to break down. We hadn't realised that Melanie had been bullied at school for her Christian faith, because she hadn't talked about it. Fortunately, after leaving school, she secured a job at a local optician and despite all the turbulence in her life, maintained her job and later went on to train and qualify as a dispensing optician. Melanie is now happily married to Graham with two beautiful children, Hope and Isaac, and we now enjoy a close relationship with her. Mel and her family attend a local church and it is such a joy to spend quality time with all the members of our family.

Mel with Hope

Mel, Graham, Hope and Isaac

Fraser kept his head down, worked hard at school and really enjoyed his music. (Melanie is very artistic and Fraser is gifted musically.) Fraser started learning piano when he was eight years old and really enjoyed this, and at twelve years old took up playing the saxophone. He practised every day without being made to do so, as he just loved music!

Fraser on the saxophone

He enjoyed many different types of music from classical to jazz. He passed grades 1-8 in piano and saxophone, and whilst at university also gained grade 8 in clarinet in a short space of time.

Music has always played a major part in Fraser's life. Whilst at senior school he entered the Hastings Music Festival most years and also was a member of Hastings Youth Jazz Orchestra, travelling to different countries with them. He also became part of a jazz band called Paplowski and whilst at Kent University, played alto saxophone and clarinet in the orchestra and concert bands. After university Fraser joined a jazz band called Swing Street and still enjoys playing saxophone with them.

For a while Fraser became a worship leader at our church and is now part of the worship team at another fellowship. Music has certainly helped him relax and keep a focus when life has been difficult. However, he was of course being affected too when our home became less than peaceful.

When Fraser was about to take his GCSE exams, his lung suddenly collapsed and he spent two weeks in Conquest Hospital whilst they tried unsuccessfully to reinflate his lung. He was then transferred to St Thomas' in London and at first it seemed he may have to undergo a very serious operation. Fortunately, after twenty-four hours there, his lung reinflated! As you can imagine, a lot of prayer had gone up... *Thank you Lord!*

Fraser was allowed to take a couple of exams at home and for the others he just went into school for the actual exam and then came home. He gradually recovered and despite being very unwell, he did amazingly, gaining eleven passes in all, with very high grades: A* in music; seven A's; two B's and one C! Fraser then went on to take A levels gaining two AS levels and two A levels. He subsequently went to Kent University in Canterbury to read Psychology and gained a 2:1 degree. Following that, he did a master's degree in Social Work at Sussex University.

During Fraser's late teens and early twenties, he also went through some very difficult times, and again it was difficult as parents to know how best to cope. We just kept trying to support Fraser as best we could and loving him.

I didn't realise it at first, but during these difficult years I had begun slipping into deep depression. I kept thinking, 'This will pass in time and I'll feel better again,' but it wasn't happening.

I found it very difficult to sleep and asked my GP if I could have some sleeping tablets. I was prescribed Zopiclone, which are very helpful in the short-term but are not meant for long-term use. In the end, I became addicted to them for fifteen years. They would give me sleep for a few hours but then I would wake and be in turmoil again.

Another very kind GP helped me very gradually to be weaned off them and now I sleep very, very well, as I have that beautiful peace of mind which Jesus gives.

I often found that being in church was the hardest place of all. I found it difficult to be in places with lots of people and I also discovered that many Christians really don't understand depression. I sensed that they were thinking, 'Why is she so depressed? Why doesn't she put some worship songs on and snap out of it?' When my depression was very severe, I was once told by a church leader that I had a spirit of suicide, in the middle of a large congregation. That leader then wouldn't talk to me or pray with me, and I went home in absolute fear that this 'spirit' would just take me over; I began to think I must need deliverance ministry.

Now that I am well, I believe this was spiritual abuse and that 'word' became a self-fulfilling prophecy. Indeed, sometime later I did make four quite serious attempts to take my own life. Then, of course, I was referred to the mental health services. I tried for a long time to work with them and found it increasingly distressing. I was sent to a local mental health day service, which I hated because again there were people there with very severe mental health difficulties and I just kept thinking, 'If I can't get better, I'll end up like them.'

I was sent to a clinic in Eastbourne where we weren't allowed to lock our rooms because we might take our own lives. But someone came into my room and stole my debit card and then used it to buy things in the town, so Geoff and I quickly had to stop my card. Another patient thought he was a horse and used to gallop up and down the corridor – I found the whole experience so frightening. There were worse 'happenings' too, but they are simply too distressing to relate. Mental Health services were trying to help me, and one particular occupational therapist who was a Christian did help and encourage me with her beautiful smile! I do not want to negate the role that medication and support from Mental Health services can give, but for me, my true healing only came about as I began to fully grasp and understand God's love.

I decided to visit Crowhurst Christian Healing Centre from time to time. I had stayed there for a few days in 1990 after my mother had died and had found that helpful. At this point, I still believed there was a god, but I certainly didn't think He loved me. I felt an utter failure with very little hope that I would ever recover. I had become very isolated and alone.

I realise it's very difficult for family and friends to know how to respond when someone suffers prolonged depression and to stick with them. A few people tried, though, and I am grateful to them.

I hated myself, and there was a growing anger inside me which I didn't know how to deal with, so mostly I turned the anger in on myself, which is so destructive. During one of my short visits to Crowhurst, I spoke to a chaplain there about my anger. He suggested we went into the small chapel with some cushions. He then left the door of the chapel slightly ajar, waited outside and gave me permission to 'bash' the cushions as hard as I wanted. I couldn't believe I'd been given permission by a chaplain to express my anger in a chapel! It helped so much and it was a tiny beginning of being able to talk about and release all the pain and hurt deep inside.

I didn't go regularly to Crowhurst but when I did, I always felt loved and accepted, however broken I was. I didn't have to pretend or put on a brave face. I could be myself and, if I needed to cry, was just given the box of tissues. I think I kept Kleenex in business! Sometimes I would have some private prayer ministry but mostly I went to the services on a Thursday morning, and very gradually, over a long period of time, I began to dare to believe that God did still love me.

The love and acceptance I experienced from 'the team' was God's love being expressed through them. How beautiful!

It was a long and sometimes very painful journey as I started to allow all the suppressed emotions of guilt, shame, unforgiveness, rejection, resentment, anger and self-hatred to come to the surface. Crowhurst was a safe place for me. Over time, and very gently and lovingly, different areas of pain were talked about and prayed into by experienced prayer ministers. Little by little, I found that I was being released and set free in a way that I had not imagined possible. The Lord was healing me from the inside out!

At Crowhurst it is taught that forgiveness is a journey – sometimes a very difficult journey. By ourselves we are not able to come to a place of total forgiveness, but what we can do is acknowledge our need of help and turn completely around to face the cross and Jesus dying on that cross to forgive us all our sin. Then He can take us by the hand and walk with us on our journey of forgiveness, step by step.

We need to be able to express all the pain and hurt as we journey and not be made to feel guilty. In Luke 22:39 we read that before the crucifixion, Jesus prayed on the mount of Olives:

> 'Father, if you are willing, take this cup from me, yet not my will but yours be done.'

Then in verse 43 we read:

> An angel from Heaven appeared to him and strengthened him – and being in anguish he prayed more earnestly and his sweat was like drops of blood falling to the ground.

Isaiah 53:3,5-6 teaches:

> He was despised and rejected by men, a man of sorrows and familiar with suffering. Like one from whom men hide their faces, he was despised. ... But he was pierced for our transgressions. He was crushed for our iniquities, the punishment that brought us peace was upon him and by his wounds we are healed. We all like sheep have gone astray, each of us turned to his own way and the LORD has laid on him the iniquity of us all.

Jesus knew deep, deep pain and suffering and He longs to help us in ours!

Recently, at a friend's funeral and thanksgiving service, the minister read from Luke 23:35 about the criminals who were being crucified at the same time as Jesus. One mocked Jesus hurling insults at Him. Verse 40 continues:

But the other criminal rebuked him saying, 'Don't you fear God, we are punished justly, but this man has done nothing wrong.' Then he said, 'Jesus, remember me when you come into your kingdom.' Jesus answered him, 'I tell you the truth, today you will be with me in paradise.'

As I meditated on these verses, I thought back over my own life and how for so many years I was trying to earn God's love, trying to please Him, not understanding His awesome grace, and that in all my struggles, He was there loving me and wanting to throw His arms around me and give me His peace.

From childhood most of us learn that if we are good, we'll have a treat, and so the concept of free unconditional love and grace takes many of us a long time to understand and accept.

For you created my inmost being, you knit me together in my mother's womb. I praise you because I am fearfully and wonderfully made, your works are wonderful I know that full well.

Psalm 139:13-14

Fear not, for I have redeemed you, I have summoned you by name, you are mine, when you pass through the waters I will be with you.

Isaiah 43:1 (emphasis added)

We are never alone.

I love many of Kari Jobe's worship songs, *I Am Not Alone* being one of them. Also, songs from her CD *The Garden* bring me right into the throne room of God.

You and I are by no means perfect – we are flawed – but the song says we are beautiful in His sight because of what Jesus accomplished for us on the cross! So we are able to come boldly to His throne of grace and receive His mercy and His love.

When I went to the communion rail in the large chapel at Crowhurst and knelt for prayer with one of the prayer ministers, I was overwhelmed as the Lord gave them beautiful pictures and words for me. So I started to keep a journal of them. Here are some given me by various prayer ministers:

- 'You are My radiant child.'
- I was a precious jewel that the Lord was holding in His hands and He was saying, 'I love you; rest in My love.'
- I was dancing and singing and full of joy. The Lord then said He wanted to keep filling me with His joy and that people would see my joy and ask where the joy came from.
- The Lord was leading me on a new pathway but would lead me step by step.
- The Lord was placing a garland of flowers on my head and delighting in me!
- The Lord was placing a crown on my head; not just a tiara, but a crown of His authority.[1]
- Jesus was taking me by the hand and looking into my eyes. He then started to pour rose petals all over me. Next he put a veil on my head to separate me for Himself. He wants me to be His bride. He loves me so much. He wants an intimate relationship with me and wants to walk with me and hold my hand as He leads me![2]

---

[1] Received 25th May 2013.
[2] Received 23rd January 2014.

- Jesus was standing in front of me smiling at me with such love in His eyes and saying that He loved me and delighted in me. After that, I was in a field of beautiful flowers and was picking the most beautiful ones. Jesus said, 'Spend much time in My presence and I will lead you and guide you to the ones I want you to give the flowers to.' He also said that He has much more for me and just as He walked this earth touching lives with His healing love and grace, so He wants to flow through my life with His healing love. A Bible verse was also given: '"Not by might, nor by power but by My spirit," says the Lord.'[3]

- There was an expensive cut glass bowl, which represented my life. As the Lord's love shone on the bowl, the many facets of the glass caused light to be reflected like beautiful rainbows.

These are just some of the beautiful words and pictures given to me. I share them because I want you to understand the depths of God's love for you too.

I echo Paul's prayer in Ephesians 3:17-21:

So that Christ may dwell in your hearts through faith and I pray that you, being rooted and established in love, may have power, together with all the saints, to grasp how wide and how long and high and deep is the love of Christ, and to know that love that surpasses knowledge, that you may be filled to the measure of all the fullness of God.

---

[3] Zechariah 4:6.

CHAPTER SEVEN

Growing Deeper in God's Love

'WITHOUT THE PAIN, I WOULDN'T BE WHO I AM TO-day.'

I was privileged to spend some time at Crowhurst when Dr Stephanie Thornton C.Psychol, AFBPsS came to share with us about the journey of forgiveness. She is a psychologist with thirty-five years of experience in studying the human mind and understanding values, attitudes and emotions. She has published many books and articles. Now retired, she converted to Catholicism while head of the psychology department at Sussex University.

I purchased Stephanie's book *Searching for Serenity – Spirituality in Later Life*[4]. I found the whole book helpful, but there was one statement that she made during the course that particularly resonated with my own heart: 'Without the pain, I wouldn't be who I am today.' And so I spoke to her about writing, as I'd been feeling for about eighteen months that I wanted to write my story. She was very encouraging, as was my pastor, Cathy Khan.

The opportunity to spend time writing came in 2016 when, following a foot operation, I had to rest for about ten weeks in

---

[4] Jim McManus, Stephanie Thornton; *Searching for Serenity – Spirituality in Later Life;* Redemptorist Publications (2010)

the summer. I used that time to start writing. I enjoyed the writing process very much. I always asked for God's help and then the writing seemed to flow.

Our daughter Melanie has also written a book entitled *Hope and Laughter* which tells of her journey to have our twin grandchildren, Hope and Isaac. Both Mel and I have enjoyed our journaling and writing but we are not so talented when it comes to maths... We all have different gifts.

Hope and Isaac at their dedication

The journey to inner wholeness can be a long one and sometimes very painful. (My journey was a long one, at least fifteen years.) We need to have courage and much love and encouragement along the way. All I can say is, it is completely worth it. I could never have imagined how beautiful my life could become, as gently and patiently Jesus led me on my healing journey. I will be eternally grateful to my Heavenly

Father and His dear son Jesus for bringing me into *this spacious place* that I now enjoy moment by moment, as my life unfolds in His precious plan!

I am also so thankful for the dear people at Crowhurst Christian Healing Centre who have loved me and supported me along my quite long and difficult journey to inner healing. That is why it is such a joy and privilege to be part of the prayer ministry team here at Crowhurst; because I know what it is like to be utterly broken. I also know that however deep the pit, God's heart of love longs to reach down and draw us up, out of the depths of despair, and set our feet in a spacious place.

> *O LORD my God, I called to you for help and you healed me.*
>
> *Psalm 30:2*

> *I will be glad and rejoice in your love, for you saw my affliction and knew the anguish of my soul you have not handed me over to the enemy but have set my feet in a <u>spacious place</u>.*
>
> *Psalm 31:7-8 (emphasis added)*

I now believe that whilst we are in those deep places of pain, our Heavenly Father is weeping over us and longing to reveal His unending mercy and grace and perfect love to us. The difficulty is that when we are in those places of brokenness, we often feel abandoned by God and cannot pray; then, when we read God's word, our perception can be so distorted that the enemy of our souls can lie to us and we can feel condemned. This is why we need people to pray for us. Make sure, however, that the people who pray for you are filled with God's compassion, mercy and grace; otherwise you may feel condemned even by Christian friends. Job's 'friends' didn't help him very much...

I love the story of the Prodigal Son. In Luke 15:20 we read:

But while he was a long way off, his father saw him and was filled with compassion for him, he ran to his son, threw his arms around him and kissed him.

That's exactly what our Heavenly Father does. Perfect, unconditional love!

We were designed to be in an intimate relationship with our Heavenly Father. It is often said there is a God-shaped hole in every person which we try to fill – an emptiness, a deep need to be loved and accepted, which I believe can only be truly filled when we discover God's perfect love for us as expressed in Jesus. All else will leave that aching void deep in our soul.

In Psalm 31:12b we read:

I have become like broken pottery.

But then verse 21 says:

Praise be to the LORD, for he has shown his wonderful love to me when I was in a besieged city. In my alarm I said, I am cut off from your sight! Yet you heard my cry for mercy when I called to you for help.

I have also found Jeremiah 30:17 encouraging:

But I will restore you to health and heal your wounds declares the LORD because you are called an outcast, Zion for whom no-one cares.

Cross made with broken pieces of pottery

Experiencing deep depression and mental ill-health can be a very lonely, isolating experience. Maybe if people haven't experienced these things themselves, it is very difficult to understand or know how to help.

But Jesus does understand.

Jesus, although fully God, was also fully man. He experienced every emotion that we experience. From the cross Jesus cried out in a loud voice, 'Eloi, Eloi, lama sabachthani?'

which means, 'My God, my God, why have you forsaken me?'[5] As Jesus took upon himself the sins of the world, He was separated from the Father for the first time.

Isaiah 53:3,5 says:

> *He was despised and rejected by men, a man of sorrows and familiar with suffering ... He was pierced for our transgressions, He was crushed for our iniquities; the punishment that brought us peace was upon him and by his wounds we are healed. We all like sheep have gone astray, each of us has turned to his own way, and the LORD has laid on Him the iniquity of us all.*

In the Gospels we see how Jesus, filled with compassion, stops for individuals. He is never too busy. Luke 4:38-41 tells of when Jesus heals Simon's mother-in-law.

> *Then when the sun was setting, the people brought to Jesus all who had various kinds of sickness and laying his hands on each one, he healed them.*

Our Heavenly Father is never too busy for us. He hears our cry and is moved with compassion.

Isaiah 61:1-3 foretells of the Messiah Jesus.

> *The Spirit of the sovereign LORD is on me because the LORD has anointed me to preach good news to the poor. He has sent me to bind up the broken hearted, to proclaim freedom for the captives, and release from darkness for the prisoners, to proclaim the year of the LORD's favour ... to comfort all who*

---

[5] See Mark 15:34.

> *mourn ... and to bestow on them a crown of beauty instead of ashes, the oil of gladness instead of mourning and a garment of praise instead of a spirit of despair.*

Then in Luke 4:14-21 we read that the scroll of the prophet Isaiah was handed to Jesus, and in verses 18 and 21 Jesus says:

> *'The Spirit of the Lord is on me, because he has anointed me to preach good news to the poor. He has sent me to proclaim freedom for the prisoners and recovery of sight for the blind, to release the oppressed, to proclaim the year of the Lord's favour. ... Today this scripture is fulfilled in your hearing.'*

Jesus the Messiah has come! He has come to make it possible for us to have that intimate relationship with our Heavenly Father. Hallelujah!

Isaac and Hope

CHAPTER EIGHT

From Mental Anguish to Peace

IN THE LARGE CHAPEL AT CROWHURST CHRISTIAN Healing Centre is a beautiful wooden cross made by Rev. Steve Clark (a former chaplain). It represents Jesus dancing through our broken world – and has some verses from Colossians 1 in the Message (MSG) translation of the Bible.

> *All the broken and dislocated pieces of the universe, people and things, animals and atoms, get properly fixed and fit together in vibrant harmonies, all because of His death, His blood that poured down from the cross.*

At one service recently another chaplain, Suzanne Owen, spoke of the art of 'Kintsukuroi', which is repairing with gold – the art of repairing pottery with gold or silver lacquer and understanding that the piece is more beautiful for having been broken.

These describe my own life so well. A Bible verse I particularly treasure is Zephaniah 3:17:

> *The LORD your God is with you,*
> *He is mighty to save.*
> *He will take great delight in you,*
> *He will quiet you with His love,*

He will rejoice over you with singing.

I enjoy every day of my life now. The Lord has filled me with His joy! I have peace – *His* peace – in my heart and my mind, and His love in my heart. Since the Lord set me free, I haven't experienced a day of depression. Every day is now a precious gift of life for me to enjoy with Him!

Some friends call me 'champagne' because I am bubbly and overflowing with God's love, joy and peace now. Some people who knew me a little when I was in deep depression and then have met me more recently have asked, 'It is Jan, isn't it?' And I reply, 'Yes, it's the wonderful Jan that my Heavenly Father has made!'

I have a beautiful relationship with my family now and they are all so thrilled at the amazing transformation that has taken place in my life. I adore my beautiful grandchildren, Hope and Isaac! Geoff and I spend much precious time with them. We have a lovely home and garden, which we share with many dear friends. Our lives are now fruitful for the Kingdom of God.

I am aware that in the future we may face other difficult times, for example when one of us dies and goes to Heaven. We are not promised a pain-free life, but we are promised that our Heavenly Father and His son Jesus will always be with us, as the precious Holy Spirit dwells within us.

I now know I am never alone and will not have to face the future alone.

Our family in 2013

Wedding anniversary, 2017

Mel and Fraser in 2015

End Note

Dear friend,

If you don't know the Lord's unconditional love for you, seek Him with all your heart because He wants to be found. He will not disappoint!

> *One thing I ask of the LORD, this is what I seek: that I may dwell in the house of the LORD all the days of my life, to gaze upon the beauty of the LORD and to seek him in his temple. For in the day of trouble he will keep me safe in his dwelling; he will hide me in the shelter of his tabernacle and set me high upon a rock. Then my head will be exalted above the enemies who surround me; at his tabernacle will I sacrifice with shouts of joy; I will sing and make music to the LORD.*
>
> *Psalm 27:4-6*

This is my prayer. Amen.

Similar Books from the Publisher

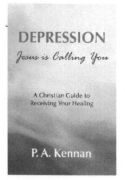

Depression – Jesus is Calling You
P. A. Kennan
ISBN 978-1-78815-665-3

What are the causes of depression? Why do some Christians struggle with anxiety, fear and confusion? Can the Bible help control our feelings? How can we break free from despair? P. A. Kennan herself struggled for many years with clinical depression, eventually leading to her contemplating suicide. However, as she began to investigate the root of her depression, she discovered a key to healing, for herself and for others.

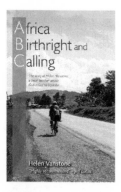

Africa, Birthright and Calling
Helen Vanstone
ISBN 978-1-78815-661-5

Helen Vanstone worked in Uganda for eight years as a voluntary head teacher at a Christian school. Earlier in her career in UK primary school education, she had faced a number of setbacks, including a poor Ofsted report, depression and bereavement. However, the opportunity in Africa turned her life around, fulfilling the calling she had received from God at a young age. Her experiences of living in a different culture and leading a school in Uganda are described with humour and honesty.